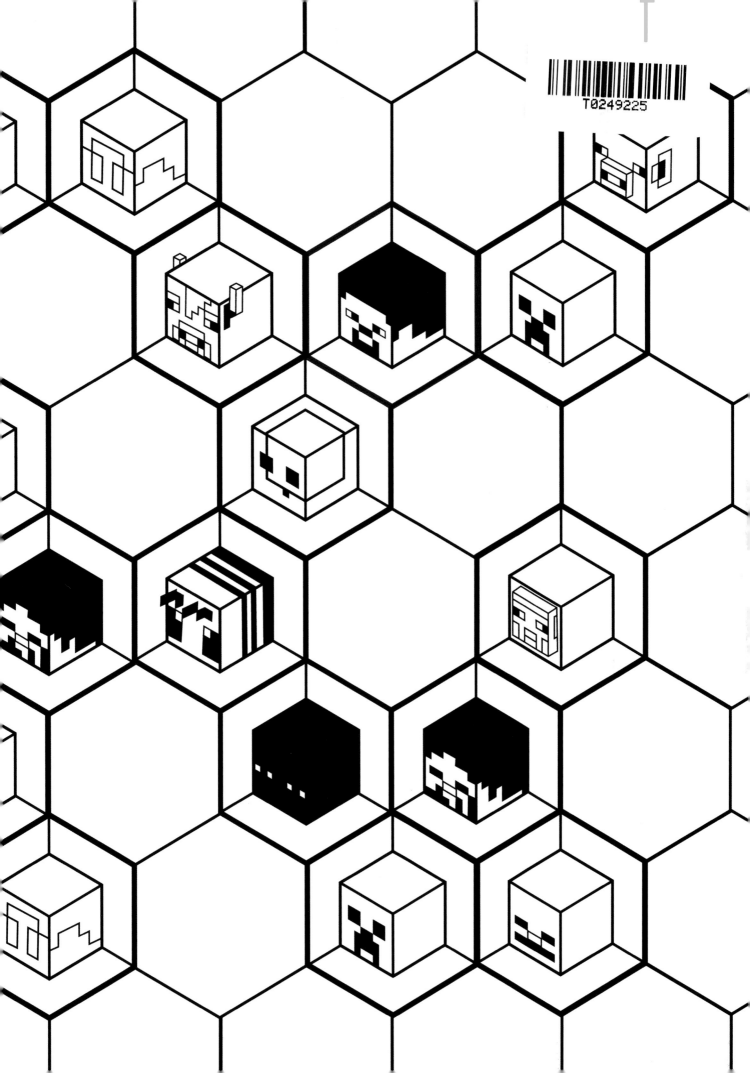

First published in Great Britain in 2024 by Farshore,
An imprint of HarperCollins*Publishers*
1 London Bridge Street, London SE1 9GF
www.farshore.co.uk

HarperCollins*Publishers*
Macken House, 39/40 Mayor Street Upper,
Dublin 1, D01 C9W8, Ireland

Special thanks to Sherin Kwan, Alex Wiltshire, Jay Castello, Kelsey Ranallo and Milo Bengtsson.

This book is an original creation by Farshore.

ISBN 978 0 00 861567 3
1
Printed and bound in Romania

**ONLINE SAFETY FOR YOUNGER FANS**

Spending time online is great fun! Here are a few simple rules to help younger fans stay safe and
keep the internet a great place to spend time:
- Never give out your real name – don't use it as your username.
- Never give out any of your personal details.
- Never tell anybody which school you go to or how old you are.
- Never tell anybody your password except a parent or a guardian.
- Be aware that you must be 13 or over to create an account on many sites.
Always check the site policy and ask a parent or guardian for permission before registering.
- Always tell a parent or guardian if something is worrying you.

Stay safe online. Any website addresses listed in this book are correct at the time of going to print.
However, Farshore is not responsible for content hosted by third parties. Please be aware that online content
can be subject to change and websites can contain content that is unsuitable for children.
We advise that all children are supervised when using the internet.

# MINECRAFT

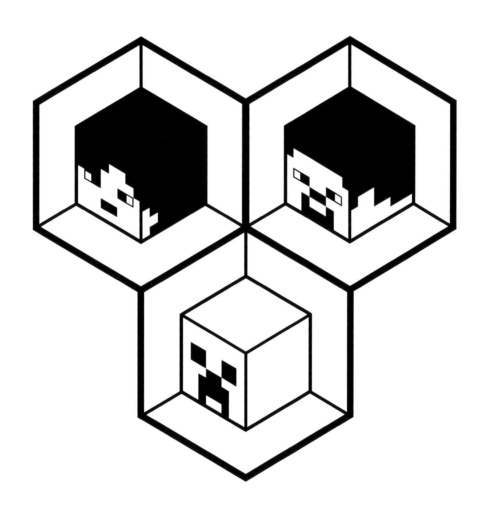

# ANNUAL 2025

# CONTENTS

20

22

48

## KEY

⬡ WORLD OF MINECRAFT

⬡ CHALLENGE

⬡ ACTIVITY

⬡ CREATE

# HELLO!

Welcome to the Minecraft Annual for 2025! This was a huge year for us as we celebrated our 15th anniversary, so we're really excited to look back at everything that's been going on, and we hope you are, too!

As usual, we've been hard at work updating Minecraft and creating new challenges, blocks and mobs for everyone to enjoy. It's like a breath of fresh air – or is that just a breeze blowing by? You have to watch out for these bushy-browed blusters in the new trial chambers, but if you're able to avoid their wind attacks and break the spawners spitting out other hostile mobs, you'll be rewarded with all kinds of treasure!

If surviving the trial chambers isn't enough excitement for you, in this book we'll explore some other challenges, such as building a new life in the Nether and collecting all 16 armour trims. We hope that the piglins like your new look! Or if building's more your style, how about making us a giant cake for our 15th birthday? If that's not enough for you, the book itself is packed with things to do, from an underwater maze to a quiz to find out which mob you're most like. Me? I'm a librarian villager, of course! There's even a board game to play with your friends, and a recipe for brownie blocks. The winner gets the biggest piece!

Whether you've been playing since the very beginning or this was your first year with Minecraft, we're so happy you're here to join us in celebrating everything we've been up to. So let's dive in!

**Jay Castello**
MOJANG STUDIOS

# A YEAR IN MINECRAFT

What an incredible year we've had in Minecraft! Not only have we spent the year partying away, celebrating Minecraft's 15th anniversary, but there have been loads of exciting new updates to explore. Let's take a look at the past year and see what's been going on, in case you missed anything.

**DISCOVER**
WITH NOOR

### 15TH ANNIVERSARY

This year, Minecraft turned a whopping 15 years old! That's 15 years full of exploring, building and updates. Did you join in any of the epic celebrations? Check out page 20 to see how the game has grown in that time.

### MINECRAFT LIVE

As always, Minecraft Live was full of exciting new updates to share with everyone. As well as seeing some of the incredible work from those in the community, we discovered a brand-new structure, a breezy hostile mob and some awesome new blocks, including the crafter. Find out more on page 10.

### MINECRAFT HIT 300 MILLION COPIES!

Over the 15 years of Minecraft, over 300 million copies of the game have been sold – WOW! To celebrate, Mojang shared some fun daily stats. On average every day, 15 million skeletons are defeated; 700 thousand cakes are made; 8.8 million pickaxes are crafted; 400 thousand wolves are tamed; 6.7 million diamonds are discovered; 915 thousand pigs are ridden; and a grand total of 0 creepers are smiling. Poor creepers – perhaps someone should give them one of those cakes!

## LO-FI TUNES

If you love Minecraft's music, then you'll want to listen to this. Mojang have released playlists of their Minecraft, Minecraft Dungeons and Minecraft Legends music with a lo-fi twist, which makes them the perfect melodies to relax, game and study with. You can find the playlists on most music platforms as well as in the Minecraft launcher.

## SNIFFERS ARE FINDING SEEDS AND STEALING HEARTS

Players have been discovering the joy of hatching their own sniffers this year. These large bumbling mobs are incredibly cute and will search for any buried seeds. Upon finding them, they plop to the ground with their legs spread out, and begin digging with their noses. Have you managed to hatch a sniffer yet?

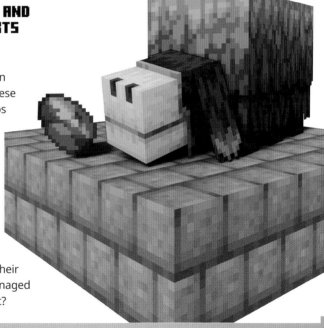

## VILLAGER ENCHANTMENTS

The enchantment books you can trade with villagers are now specific to which biome the villager is from. So if you're looking for a specific enchantment, you'll now need to find the correct villager to get it.

## TRICKY TRIALS UPDATE

The latest update has added all kinds of exciting new adventures to the game, including the challenging trial chambers. Unlike anything else you've ever seen in the game, you'll discover plenty of new blocks, mobs and trials inside. Have you explored one yet? Check out what else has been added on page 36.

## DECORATED POT STORAGE

Now decorated pots are more than just pretty decorations – you can hide things in them! They can store up to 64 items in a single stack.

# MINECRAFT LIVE

One of the most highly anticipated moments for Minecraft fans each year, Minecraft Live is an annual celebration of the community and a chance to discover what new things are coming. And, of course, you can't forget the mob vote! Did you tune in last year? If not, don't worry, let's catch you up!

## TRICKY TRIALS UPDATE

Mojang clued us in on just a fraction of the exciting things to come in the next update. From trial chambers, trial spawners and a new hostile mob: the breeze, to new copper blocks and the crafter, it's safe to say that what they shared was enough to get everyone excited for this update.

# ARMADILLO FACT FILE

As usual, this year there were three exciting new mobs to choose from: the crab, penguin or armadillo. After all the votes were cast, it was the armadillo that came out victorious! Here's all you need to know about the cutest new mob to join the Overworld!

Found two armadillos? Feed them both spider eyes and they'll breed an armadillo pup. Cute!

Got some spider eyes in your inventory? Get them out and a nearby armadillo will follow you.

## MOB NOTES

**BEHAVIOUR:** This passive mob will roll up into a ball if it gets hurt, protecting itself from taking as much damage. Spiders will avoid it, so it's a handy creature to keep close by when the sun goes down!

**DROPS:** This mob drops armadillo scutes, but there's no need to defeat the little guy – just give it a brush or bide your time and it will drop one and be on its merry way!

You can speed up the growth time of an armadillo pup by feeding it spider eyes, too. Basically, if you like armadillos, find some spider eyes!

## HABITAT
Armadillos are most commonly found in savanna biomes, where they spawn in groups of two to three. However, if you're lucky, you'll also spot one or two in badland biomes, too!

Armadillo scutes can be crafted into armour to protect your trusty pet wolf! You'll need six scutes to craft it.

# SURVIVAL CHALLENGE
## LIVE IN THE NETHER

**SURVIVE**
WITH SUNNY

Ahh, the Nether. Home to terrifying mobs, perilous drops and lava pools aplenty. The perfect place to settle down, right? Don't let the limited cuisine and anti-social neighbours put you off — there are loads of local treasures to fill your base with. So pack your inventory and let's go on a new adventure to the Nether!

### 1 WHAT TO PACK

Though you can find most things you need in the Nether if you look hard enough, you may find it difficult to survive long enough to locate them all, so it's best to pack your bags first. Be sure to leave some slots left for all the amazing treasures you'll find, but stuff your inventory with the following things: wood, food, weapons and tools (including a diamond pickaxe), a saddle, a hopper and a fishing rod. Also equip yourself at least one piece of gold armour.

### 2 FIRST THINGS FIRST

As soon as you land in the Nether, quickly assess your surroundings. Which biome are you in? How close to falling in lava or off a cliff are you? Are there any mobs about to attack you? If you're lucky and relatively safe, then now's a good time to scout around for as much gold ore as you can. Gold ingots will be invaluable for trading with piglins for cool stuff later.

### 3 THE FLOOR IS LAVA

You're never far from a lava pool in the Nether, and sometimes walking around them or bridging over them is not an option. Thankfully, there is a super-cute solution to that issue! The strider is the only passive mob you'll find in the Nether, so treat it well! You can saddle it up and steer it by dangling its favourite food – warped fungus – in front of it with a fishing rod.

### THE PRICE IS RIGHT
**4** Before long, you'll stumble across a piglin, whether you're infiltrating a bastion remnant or Nether fortress, or out roaming around the biomes. These are neutral mobs, but only if you're wearing a piece of gold. If you are suitably dressed, then you can barter with a piglin by giving them a gold ingot. They'll then toss you an item in return – awesome!

### GHASTLY CRYING
**5** If you hear something that sounds almost like a yawning cat, followed by a terrifying screech, duck! A ghast has just launched a fireball at you. These ghost-like floating mobs spawn in the soul sand valley, basalt deltas and Nether wastes biomes, so keep watch in these areas. If you defeat a ghast, it will drop a ghast tear, which can be used to make the potion of Regeneration.

### BONE AS OLD AS TIME
**6** In the soul sand valley biome, you might come across a huge fossil structure, that looks like the bones of a massive prehistoric beasty! They're a pretty cool sight to behold!

### BASTION REMNANT
**7** One of the two structures you'll find in the Nether, the bastion remnant is home to all manner of treasures (if you're lucky!), including the snout smithing template and banner pattern, as well as crying obsidian, a Pigstep music disc and the netherite upgrade smithing template. There are plenty of chests dotted about to loot, so see what you can find! But be wary, with great loot comes great danger: piglin brutes, with their big golden belt buckles, will not be appeased by gold – they will attack at first sight, so be sure to keep a weapon at the ready.

### 8 SNEAKY THIEF

Unsurprisingly, piglins don't like it when you steal from them – who would? So if you open a chest in a bastion remnant or Nether fortress, you'll have a piglin or two to answer to. But what if you don't want to fight off a bunch of piglins? This is where you can get sneaky. Remember that hopper you packed? Dig out the block below a chest and place the hopper there to take all the items out of the chest without alerting the piglins to your thieving. Genius!

### 9 NETHER FORTRESS

If you wish to become a brewing wizard, then you'll want to explore this structure. It's home to blazes, a mob with a fiery temper that drops blaze rods when defeated. These are an essential ingredient for crafting a brewing stand – or eyes of Ender, should you wish to locate a stronghold. The fortress is also where you'll find Nether wart – which is an important potion ingredient – as well as the rib smithing template and a bunch of other loot.

### 10 ANCHOR DOWN

Once you've been in the Nether long enough, you'll notice that there's no sun there, which means there's no daylight cycle. And if endless darkness didn't sound bad enough, you won't be able to sleep through any of it as beds explode if you place them in the Nether! But what if you want to set a respawn location there? Then you'll need to collect yourself enough crying obsidian and glowstones to craft yourself a respawn anchor.

## 11 TOUGH STUFF

If you're looking for the strongest tools and armour, then you'll want to get your hands on some netherite and the netherite upgrade smithing template to apply to your diamond armour. You can loot structures for netherite scraps or you can mine deep down to find some ancient debris, which is the ore for netherite.

## 12 FEELING PECKISH

Have you run out of food already? Then you've got two options, either build yourself a portal back to the Overworld to collect more grub, or take your chances with a hoglin. A source of porkchops – one of the very limited foods options in the Nether – you can bet that these mobs don't go down easy! Unlike the friendly pigs in the Overworld, hoglins will put up a good fight.

## 13 HOT TOURIST DESTINATION

If you're a true explorer, you'll want this achievement. Just visit all five Nether biomes: soul sand valley, basalt deltas, crimson forest, warped forest and Nether wastes.

# SPOT THE DIFFERENCE
# CHERRY GROVE

Ari and Kai have set up camp for the night in a cherry grove, after a long day of exploring. It might be the flickering flames of the campfire or perhaps their tiredness and hunger are affecting their eyesight, but things seem to be shifting around them. Can you see it, too? Spot the ten differences between the scenes and tick them off below.

1 ◯  2 ◯  3 ◯  4 ◯  5 ◯  6 ◯  7 ◯  8 ◯  9 ◯  10 ◯

# ARMOUR TRIMS

Structures got some new loot in 2023 with the addition of armour trims. With 16 smithing templates, 6 materials and 10 crystals/ingots to use across 4 pieces of armour, there are thousands of different combinations you can create with armour trims. Sure, they provide no extra protection, but how awesome do they look?!

## ARMOUR MATERIALS

All of these materials can have trims added to them.

LEATHER

GOLD

CHAINMAIL

IRON

DIAMOND

NETHERITE

## TRIM MATERIALS

These are what you'll use with the smithing template to add trims in various colours to your armour.

| | | | |
|---|---|---|---|
| AMETHYST |  |  | QUARTZ |
| COPPER |  |  | IRON |
| DIAMOND |  |  | LAPIS LAZULI |
| EMERALD |  |  | NETHERITE |
| GOLD |  |  | REDSTONE |

**TOP TIP!** You can even use the same crystal or ingot to add a trim to armour of the same material – the pattern will just appear as a darker shade.

## SMITHING TEMPLATES

To add armour trims, you'll need to use a smithing table, and combine together a smithing template, a crystal or an ingot and a piece of armour. Be warned, smithing templates are rare and they can only be used once, so take care of your fancy new armour trims.

Upgrade Gear

## COAST

**FOUND:** shipwrecks
**GENERATION:** 2 in chests, randomly
**DUPLICATION BLOCK:** cobblestone

## DUNE
**FOUND:** desert temples
**GENERATION:** 2 in chests, randomly
**DUPLICATION BLOCK:** sandstone

## EYE
**FOUND:** strongholds,
**GENERATION:** 1 in altar chests, randomly and 1 in library chests
**DUPLICATION BLOCK:** End stone

## HOST
**FOUND:** trail ruins
**GENERATION:** 1 in suspicious gravel, randomly
**DUPLICATION BLOCK:** terracotta

## RAISER
**FOUND:** trail ruins
**GENERATION:** 1 in suspicious gravel, randomly
**DUPLICATION BLOCK:** terracotta

## RIB
**FOUND:** Nether fortresses
**GENERATION:** 1 in chests, randomly
**DUPLICATION BLOCK:** netherrack

## SENTRY
**FOUND:** pillager outposts
**GENERATION:** 2 in chests, randomly
**DUPLICATION BLOCK:** cobblestone

## SHAPER
**FOUND:** trail ruins
**GENERATION:** 1 in suspicious gravel, randomly
**DUPLICATION BLOCK:** terracotta

## SILENCE
**FOUND:** ancient cities
**GENERATION:** 1 in chests, randomly
**DUPLICATION BLOCK:** cobbled deepslate

## SNOUT
**FOUND:** bastion remnants
**GENERATION:** 1 in chests, randomly
**DUPLICATION BLOCK:** blackstone

## SPIRE
**FOUND:** End cities
**GENERATION:** 1 in chests, randomly
**DUPLICATION BLOCK:** purpur

## TIDE
**FOUND:** ocean monuments
**GENERATION:** elder guardians randomly drop 1 when defeated
**DUPLICATION BLOCK:** prismarine

## VEX
**FOUND:** woodland mansions
**GENERATION:** 1 in chests, randomly
**DUPLICATION BLOCK:** cobblestone

## WARD
**FOUND:** ancient cities
**GENERATION:** 1 in chests, randomly
**DUPLICATION BLOCK:** cobbled deepslate

## WAYFINDER
**FOUND:** trail ruins
**GENERATION:** 1 in suspicious gravel, randomly
**DUPLICATION BLOCK:** terracotta

## WILD
**FOUND:** jungle temples
**GENERATION:** 2 in chests, randomly
**DUPLICATION BLOCK:** mossy cobblestone

# 15 YEARS OF MINECRAFT

Can you believe Minecraft turned 15 years old this year? Every year, the game has gotten bigger and bigger with new things being added. Let's take a look back at the journey Minecraft has been on so far and some of the awesome things that have been added to the game along the way.

**DISCOVER WITH NOOR**

## THE BIRTH OF MINECRAFT!

Not only was this the year the game was born, but also the year that Minecrafters came into being! Did you play it back then?

## ADVENTURE UPDATE

This update added some exciting new structures for explorers to discover, such as villages, strongholds and mineshafts, plus the End dimension! And of course these did not come uninhabited – villagers, Endermen, silverfish and cave spiders were also added this year.

## PRETTY SCARY UPDATE

As the name suggests, this update came with some pretty terrifying new mobs, such as the Wither, Wither skeletons, witches and zombie villagers – ARGH!

## THE COMBAT UPDATE

This year, the End received an upgrade, adding its outer islands, along with End cities, shulkers, chorus trees and quite possibly the most exciting loot of the game: elytra. Who doesn't want to fly?!

**2009  2010  2011  2012  2013  2014  2015  2016**

## NETHER WAS BORN

Only a year after the Overworld came into existence, the Nether was added to the game, along with some ghastly mobs that still reside there today!

## HORSE UPDATE

You guessed it: this update saw the introduction of horses to the game. It also added donkeys, mules, skeleton horses and zombie horses, so you'd never need to walk across the Overworld again!

## BOUNTIFUL UPDATE

Say hello to Alex! It's hard to imagine Steve without Alex, but he had five lonely years before her addition to the game. But she wasn't the only upgrade that year – ocean monuments, along with their many blocks and guardians were also added. Plus rabbits – because why not?

## EXPLORATION UPDATE

Woodland mansions were introduced to the Overworld in this update, along with their grumpy residents: vindicators, evokers and vexes. On the bright side, we also got llamas this year!

# 15 YEARS

## WORLD OF COLOUR UPDATE

Indeed, this update brought plenty of colourful blocks to the Overworld with the introduction of coloured concrete and concrete powder, as well as glazed terracotta and the ability to dye beds. Plus they added parrots to the game!

## VILLAGE & PILLAGE

This was both an exciting and terrifying year for villagers. While they gained a purpose in the form of new jobs, they also gained a new foe in the form of pillagers. Since then, if a player enters their peaceful village with the Bad Omen effect, waves of illagers arrive to attack them. EEK!

## NETHER UPDATE

As if the Nether wasn't already terrifying enough, this update filled it with a whole host of new residents from piglins, hoglins and zoglins to (admittedly quite cute) striders. At least the new biomes and addition of netherite are pretty awesome!

## TRAILS & TALES

This was an exciting update for intrepid explorers: not only was archaeology introduced to the game, but also smithing templates. Plus who doesn't love the stunning new cherry grove biome and camels?!

| 2017 | 2018 | 2019 | 2020 | 2021 | 2022 | 2023 | 2024 |
|------|------|------|------|------|------|------|------|

## UPDATE AQUATIC

Suddenly diving beneath the ocean got a lot more exciting with the addition of plenty of new marine mobs, plus shipwrecks and buried treasure, so that you could go on some new pirate adventures.

## CAVES AND CLIFFS

Underground got a lot more magical in this update. With the introduction of different cave types, including lush caves, we got to meet an adorable new mob: the axolotl. As well as goats and glow squids!

## TRICKY TRIALS

Which leads up to this last year, when we got to tackle a new challenge in the form of the trial chambers. This dangerous treasure trove is sure to keep explorers on their toes for many years to come.

## THE WILD UPDATE

This update was toad-ally awesome as well as utterly terrifying. The fearsome frog and mega-cute warden were added to the game ... wait, that's not right! They also came with their own new habitats: the mangrove swamp and deep dark.

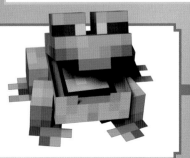

# BUILD CHALLENGE
## ANNIVERSARY CAKE BASE

**BUILDING**
WITH KAI

Celebrate Minecraft's 15th birthday with us by crafting this scrumptious-looking cake base! This build will see friends turning up on your doorstep – plus a few zombies – all hungry for cake (and brains)! Let's get eating – I mean – building!

**DIFFICULTY:**
★★☆☆☆
🕐 25 mins

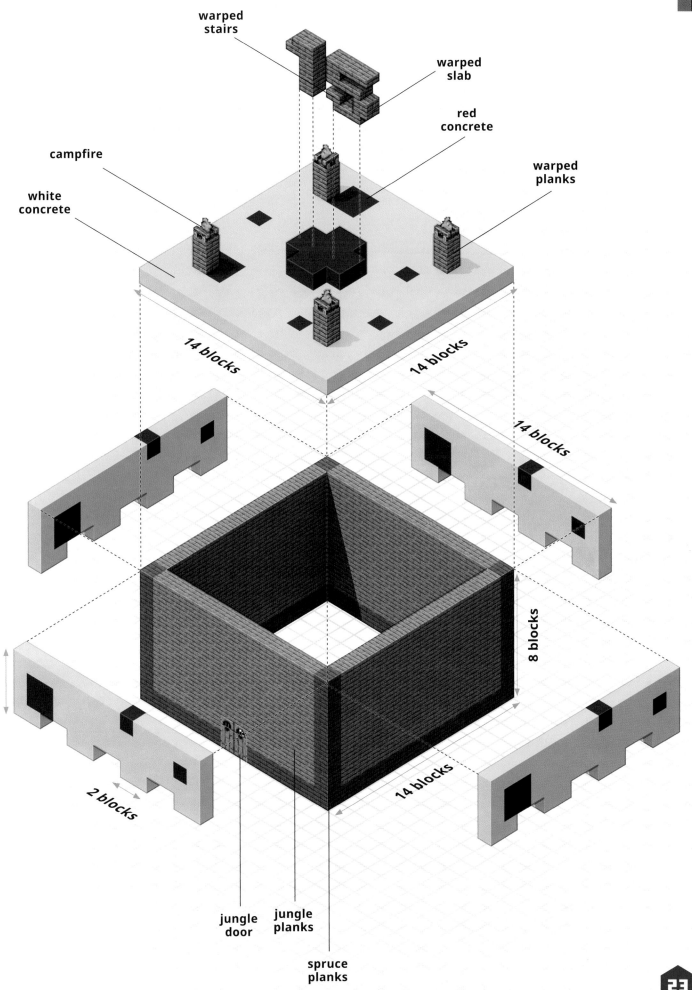

warped
stairs

warped
slab

red
concrete

campfire

white
concrete

warped
planks

14 blocks

14 blocks

14 blocks

4 blocks

8 blocks

2 blocks

14 blocks

jungle
door

jungle
planks

spruce
planks

# MINECRAFT MAZE
# OCEAN FLOOR

PUZZLES WITH STEVE

Makena and Ari are on an underwater treasure hunt. Can you help them find their way across the ocean floor to an ocean monument? You'll need to be quick, though – they forgot to pack their turtle helmets! Be sure to avoid the guardians and elder guardians.

START

FINISH

Check your answers on page 68

# REMINISCE WITH MOJANG STUDIOS

**DISCOVER**
WITH NOOR

It's been 15 years of Minecraft and in that time, the game has become HUGE with hundreds of blocks, dozens of mobs and various biomes and game modes. With so many things to choose from, figuring out your favourite thing about Minecraft can be a difficult task indeed! Let's see what the creators at Mojang love the most. Do you agree?

## MAGMA CUBE

### JENS BERGENSTEN, CHIEF CREATIVE OFFICER

I love the magma cube. It looks and sounds funny, and feels genuinely 'Minecraft-y' as a creature.

## GHAST

### ANNA LUNDGREN, PRODUCER

I just love the ghast, the eerie feeling when you enter the Nether and hear a ghast make almost giggling noises is priceless! The fact that they are both very cute and very dangerous makes them even more interesting.

## NETHER

### MATT GARTZKE, COMMUNITY MANAGER

I love the warped forests that were added with the Nether Update! I've tried to build a homestead in the area on several occasions, but every time, a ghast flies in and ruins the fun.

## EXPLORING NEW WORLDS

### JASPER BOESTRA, ART DIRECTOR

My favourite thing in Minecraft is starting a new world with my friends and searching for a spot to settle in. During this big adventure, we'll travel for a long time and run into all kinds of trouble – mostly losing each other or debating whether to stay here or continue!

## BUILDING A TOWN

### DAVID CARLTON, DEVELOPER LEAD, MINECRAFT REALMS

My favourite thing in Minecraft is building a town with my friends. We'll go on adventures, exploring and collecting exciting things to bring back, and make homes that are impressive but also expressive of each of our personalities. There's always a story to tell, like a castle with gilded blackstone accents.

## COLOURS

### KRISTINA HORNER, COMMUNITY MANAGER

I love anything in-game that can be dyed all colours of the rainbow. From concrete to pet collars to stained glass, I try to make every build I create as colourful as possible. My crowning glory is my rainbow sheep farm, complete with a series of auto sheep-shearing machines that provide me with all the colourful wool I could possibly need!

# REMINISCE WITH MOJANG

## FOX

### CAMERON THOMAS, SENIOR COMMUNITY MANAGER

My favourite mob in Minecraft is the fox! Admittedly, I think real foxes are awesome, too, but in Minecraft, they're even cuter. You can actually befriend them and they don't leave your driveway littered with rubbish in the morning after you put the bins out for collection the night before. What's not to love?

## STORYTELLING

### AGNES LARSSON, GAME DIRECTOR

My favourite way to play Minecraft is as a world builder and storyteller. By using Minecraft and my imagination, I create multiple kingdoms with family legacies lasting over multiple generations, as well as villages and cities with different shops, residential and cultural buildings.

## CATS

### MARIANA SALIMENA PIRES, SENIOR CONCEPT ARTIST

My favourite thing in Minecraft – and also in real life – is the cats! I love going on an adventure to find a cat in a nearby village, slowly charming it with food to eventually turn it into my pet and give it a name tag with a funny name. My current Minecraft pet is a black cat named Cookie, who lives with me inside my mushroom house.

## MUSIC

### JAY WELLS, COMMUNITY MANAGER

If I had to choose one of my favourite things, I would probably say it's the music. The soundtrack that plays when I'm exploring the End dimension always gives me shivers, and I have such great memories of adventures I've had in the Nether dimension with the atmospheric tracks playing in the background.

## EARLY-GAME SURVIVAL

### JOSH MULANAX, RELEASE MANAGER

My favourite thing about Minecraft is a fresh survival world with friends. The possibilities for adventure are endless and we never quite know what trouble we'll be getting into! We always start a new world with each big gameplay update and try to find the new stuff as fast as possible to see how it changes up the way we build a base and explore the rest of the world.

## BUILDING BASES

### MARC WATSON, PRODUCER

My favourite thing in Minecraft has got to be setting up a functional base that my friends and I can enjoy. From building fishing piers to planting crops to levelling up villager trades, getting everything working smoothly is a priority. The more efficient we can be with resupplying, the sooner we can get back to adventuring!

## BRANCH MINING

### ADRIAN ÖSTERGÅRD, PRODUCER FOR MUSIC & AUDIO

One of my favourite things in Minecraft is branch mining. There's something weirdly therapeutic about it. The constant back and forth through your branches while hearing the familiar block-breaking sounds, and the small dopamine hits when you find diamonds is so satisfying. Combining this with either the Minecraft soundtrack or your favourite tunes puts me in such a good mood.

# BUILD CHALLENGE
## BAMBOO CRAFTER

**BUILDING** WITH KAI

Want to speed up your bamboo builds in Survival mode? Try out this automatic bamboo crafter! This contraption will harvest your bamboo and send it straight down into a crafter, where it will craft blocks of bamboo for you. Want to build a bamboo house in a jiffy? This will help! Want an endless supply of bamboo rafts? Consider it done!

**DIFFICULTY:**
★★★☆☆
🕐 35 mins

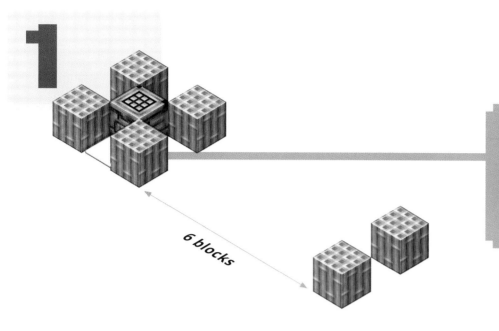

**1**

*6 blocks*

Start by placing a crafter with an iron pressure plate in front of it. The pressure plate will trigger the crafter to start crafting when you stand on it. Add 1 block of bamboo on each corner of the crafter, then add 2 more, 7 blocks to the right.

**2**

Pop a hopper on top of your crafter, then add another layer to all your blocks of bamboo. Using more blocks of bamboo, fill in the spaces in between your pillars, leaving the space above the pressure plate free.

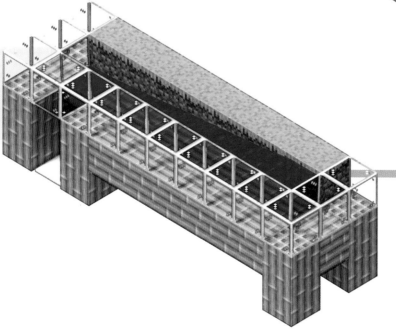

**3**

At the back of your build, add a row of grass blocks, leaving a block free on either end. Use glass blocks to complete a loop with the grass around the top of the build. At the opposite end to the hopper, add 1 water source block in the gap. This will send anything that lands in it flowing down to the hopper and into the crafter.

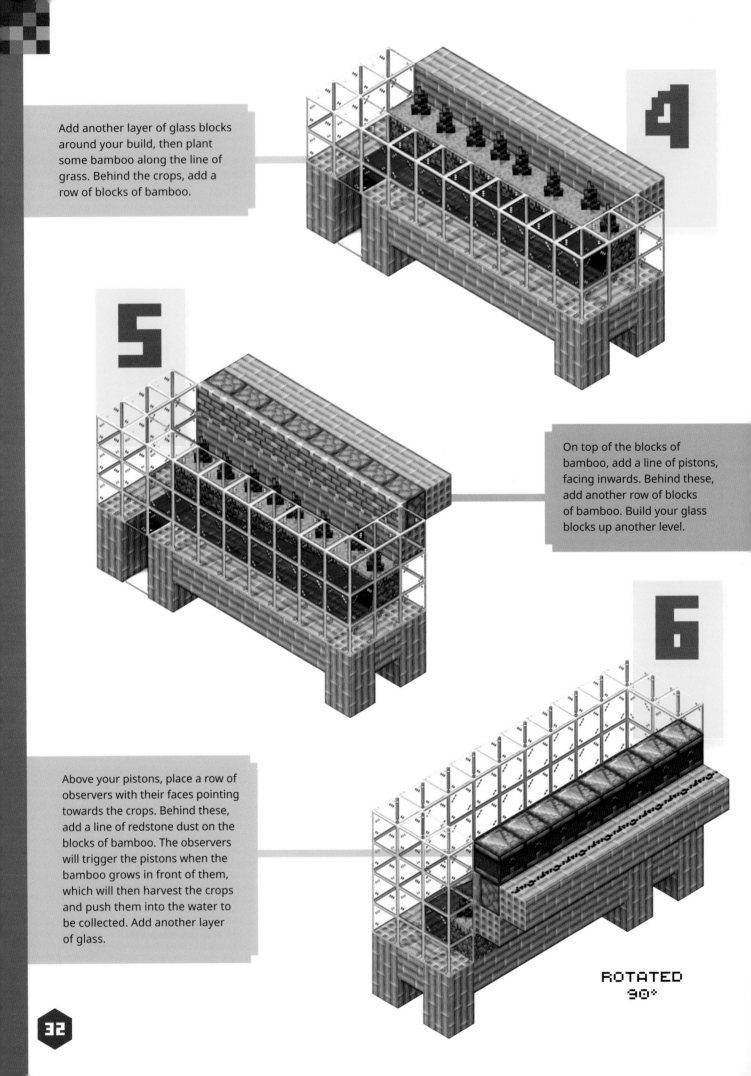

Add another layer of glass blocks around your build, then plant some bamboo along the line of grass. Behind the crops, add a row of blocks of bamboo.

4

5

On top of the blocks of bamboo, add a line of pistons, facing inwards. Behind these, add another row of blocks of bamboo. Build your glass blocks up another level.

6

Above your pistons, place a row of observers with their faces pointing towards the crops. Behind these, add a line of redstone dust on the blocks of bamboo. The observers will trigger the pistons when the bamboo grows in front of them, which will then harvest the crops and push them into the water to be collected. Add another layer of glass.

ROTATED
90°

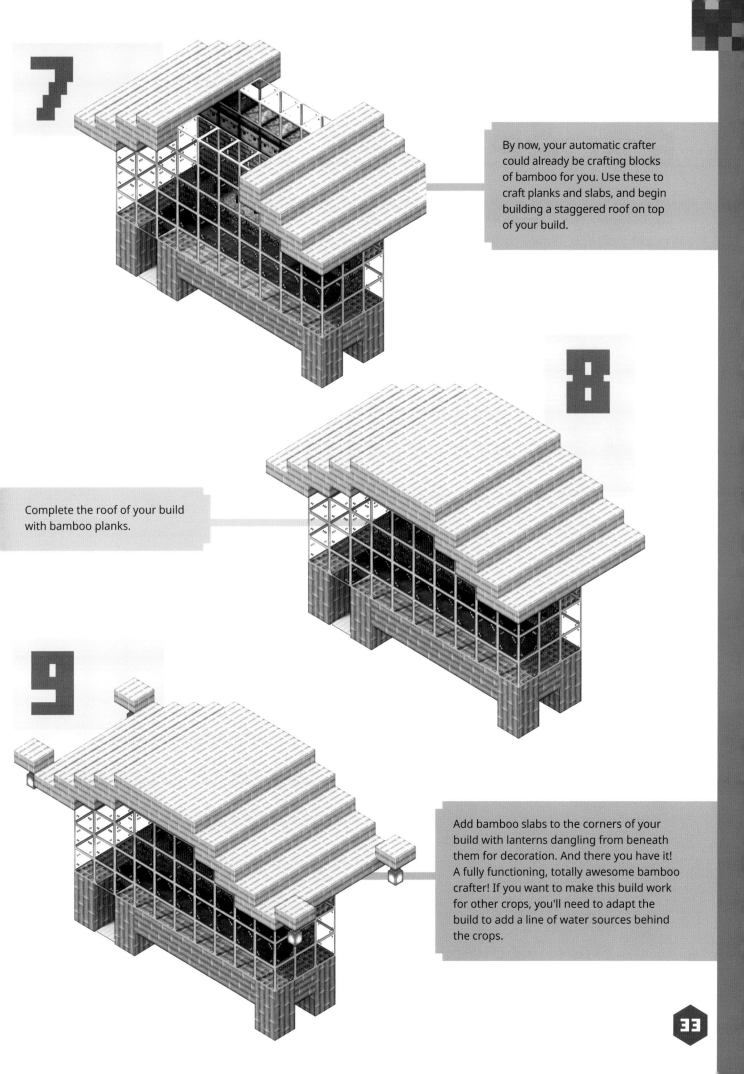

**7**

By now, your automatic crafter could already be crafting blocks of bamboo for you. Use these to craft planks and slabs, and begin building a staggered roof on top of your build.

**8**

Complete the roof of your build with bamboo planks.

**9**

Add bamboo slabs to the corners of your build with lanterns dangling from beneath them for decoration. And there you have it! A fully functioning, totally awesome bamboo crafter! If you want to make this build work for other crops, you'll need to adapt the build to add a line of water sources behind the crops.

# BOARD GAME
## ESCAPE THE MINE!

Grab your dice and some mates, and let's play a board game together. Race to the exit, avoiding all the hazards. Will you be fortunate enough to make it to the end unscathed, or will you fall victim to the lava, holes and hostile mobs lurking in the dark?

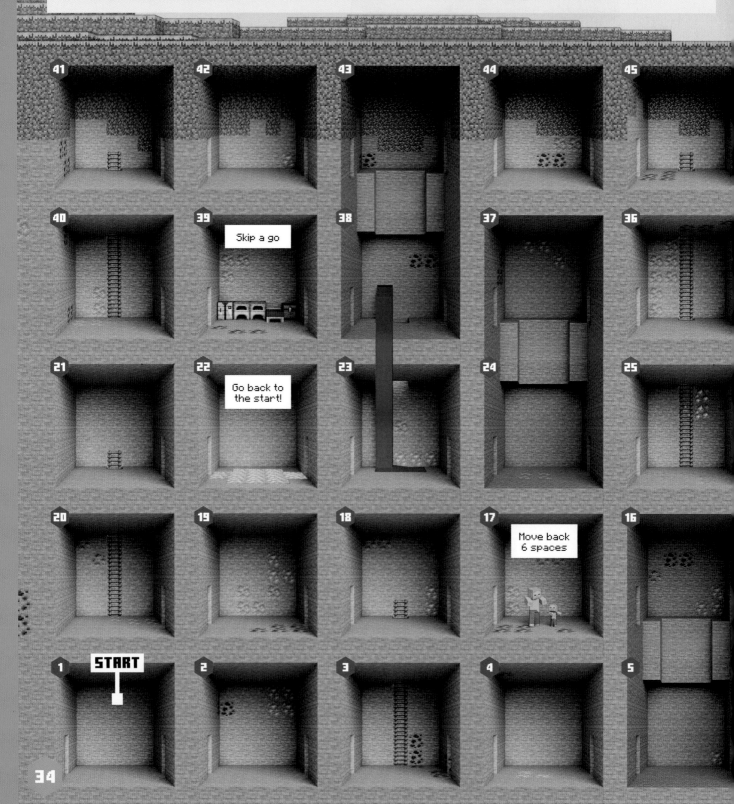

34

# RULES

**YOU WILL NEED:**
- 2+ players
- 2 dice
- A counter each (you can make these yourself!)

**1.** Roll both dice and move forward how many steps you get.
**2.** If you stumble across a lava lake, you'll have to return to the start! If you come head-to-head with a hostile mob, move back the stated number of spaces. If you land in a hole, fall down to the space beneath.
**3.** If you land on a ladder, climb to the top. If you get a waterfall, swim on up to the top of it!
**4.** If you move to a bed, have a quick nap and skip your next go.
**5.** The winner is the first person to make it out of the mine!

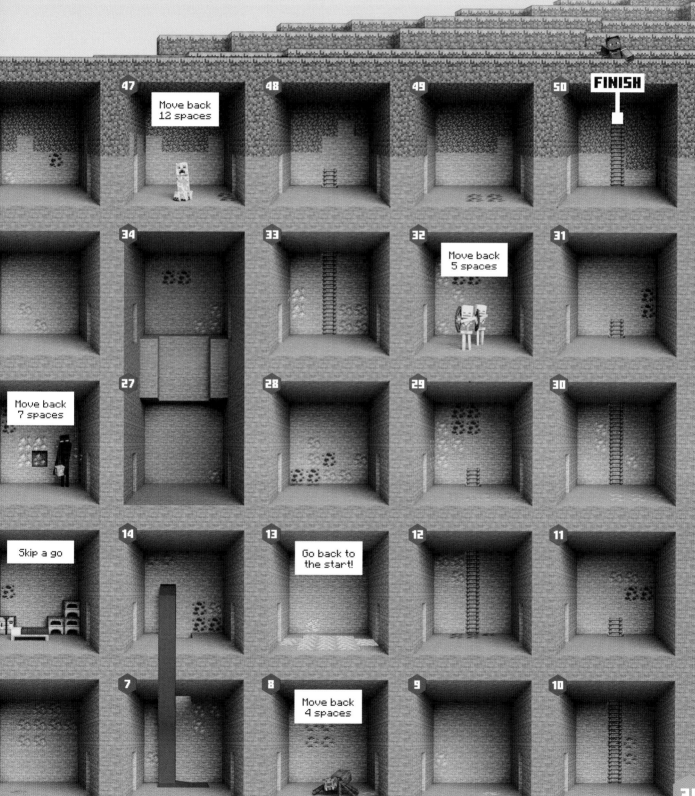

| 47 | 48 | 49 | 50 |
|----|----|----|----|
| Move back 12 spaces | | | FINISH |

| 34 | 33 | 32 | 31 |
|----|----|----|----|
| | | Move back 5 spaces | |

| 27 | 28 | 29 | 30 |
|----|----|----|----|
| Move back 7 spaces | | | |

| 14 | 13 | 12 | 11 |
|----|----|----|----|
| Skip a go | Go back to the start! | | |

| 7 | 8 | 9 | 10 |
|----|----|----|----|
| | Move back 4 spaces | | |

35

# TRICKY TRIALS UPDATE

Grab some friends and armour up — this next update is a wild adventure. Whether you're a fan of multiplayer journeys, survival challenges or creating awesome redstone contraptions, this update has something to excite every player! How many things have you already discovered?

**UPDATES**
WITH ALEX

## TRIAL CHAMBERS

Located underground, this structure is full of corridors, leading to chambers filled with different trials and challenges. These rooms can contain anything from chests full of loot to trial spawners that unleash a horde of hostile mobs on you. Are you brave enough to accept the challenge?

## THE BREEZE

While exploring the trial chambers, you may come across a new hostile mob, the breeze. This mischievous mob will whirl around, attacking you with bursts of energy called wind charges. Not only will these wind charges cause you damage if they directly hit you, but they can also interact with other elements in the room, such as trapdoors, turning the room against you. Defeat a breeze, though, and you could pick up a wind charge of your own to play with!

## ARMADILLO

This mob may look cute and harmless, but while we run from spiders, spiders are running from armadillos! That's because this mob eats spider eyes for breakfast (and lunch and dinner!). Watch out spiders – they're coming for you!

## CRAFTER

If you love redstone, you'll no doubt have already spent loads of time playing with this new block. With the use of the crafter, you can automate crafting. Just fill it with materials and select a recipe to craft, and it will craft items or blocks at the press of a button until you run out of materials inside. What will you have it craft?

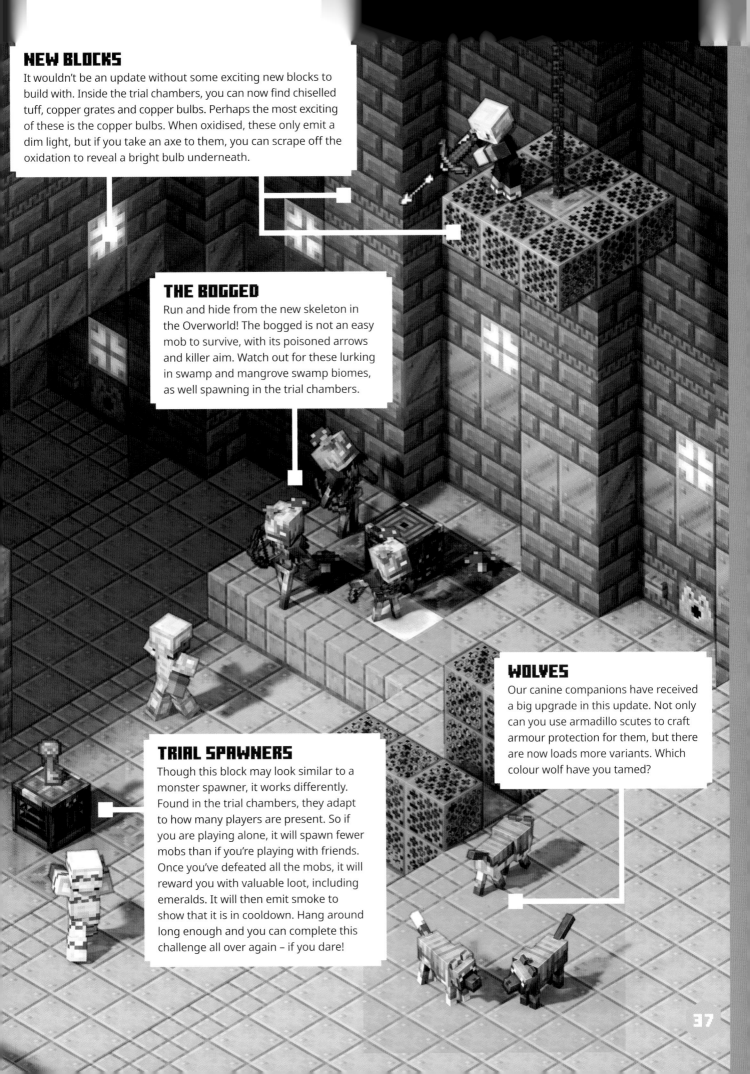

## NEW BLOCKS

It wouldn't be an update without some exciting new blocks to build with. Inside the trial chambers, you can now find chiselled tuff, copper grates and copper bulbs. Perhaps the most exciting of these is the copper bulbs. When oxidised, these only emit a dim light, but if you take an axe to them, you can scrape off the oxidation to reveal a bright bulb underneath.

## THE BOGGED

Run and hide from the new skeleton in the Overworld! The bogged is not an easy mob to survive, with its poisoned arrows and killer aim. Watch out for these lurking in swamp and mangrove swamp biomes, as well spawning in the trial chambers.

## WOLVES

Our canine companions have received a big upgrade in this update. Not only can you use armadillo scutes to craft armour protection for them, but there are now loads more variants. Which colour wolf have you tamed?

## TRIAL SPAWNERS

Though this block may look similar to a monster spawner, it works differently. Found in the trial chambers, they adapt to how many players are present. So if you are playing alone, it will spawn fewer mobs than if you're playing with friends. Once you've defeated all the mobs, it will reward you with valuable loot, including emeralds. It will then emit smoke to show that it is in cooldown. Hang around long enough and you can complete this challenge all over again – if you dare!

# BUILD CHALLENGE
## NETHER PORTAL LANTERN

**BUILDING** WITH KAI

Argh! Your portal has opened up way up high in the Nether! You could build some stairs going down from it ... or you could embrace the heights and turn it into a dangling portal lantern! Pop on your elytra and soar down from above – just don't land in lava!

**DIFFICULTY:**
★★☆☆☆
🕐 25 mins

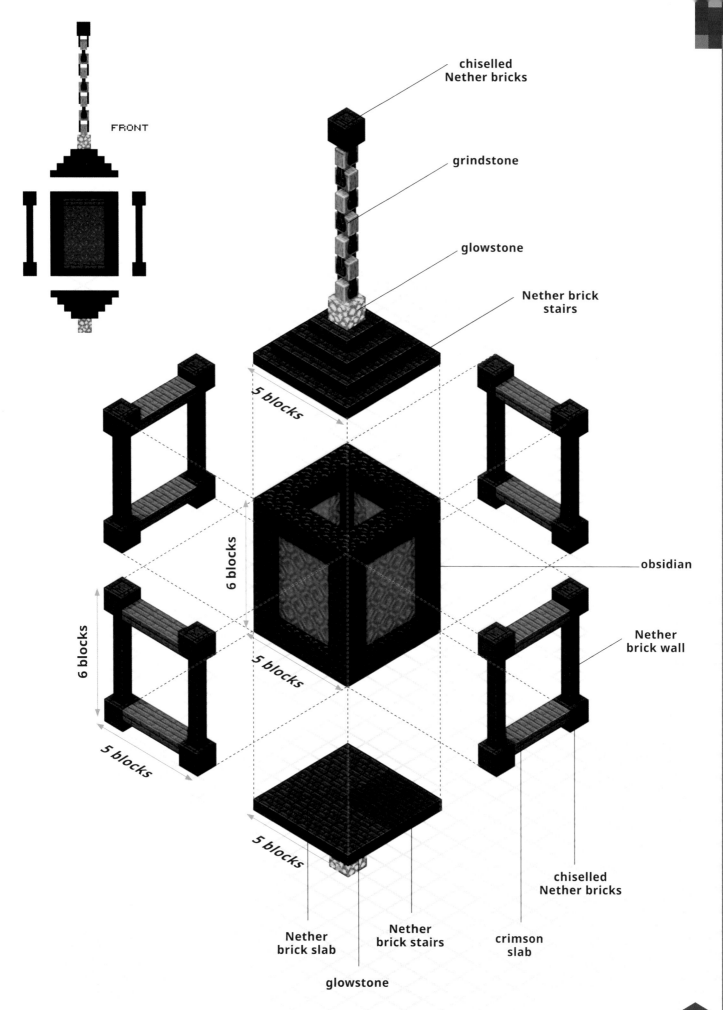

FRONT

chiselled
Nether bricks

grindstone

glowstone

Nether brick
stairs

5 blocks

6 blocks

obsidian

6 blocks

5 blocks

Nether
brick wall

6 blocks

5 blocks

5 blocks

chiselled
Nether bricks

Nether
brick slab

Nether
brick stairs

crimson
slab

glowstone

# WHICH MOB ARE YOU?

Ever wondered which mob you'd be in Minecraft? Take this quiz and discover which mob is most like you! Are you a shy Enderman who likes to keep to themself, or a helpful allay who is always there for a friend? Let's find out in the quiz below!

**PUZZLES**
WITH STEVE

## 1 When your alarm goes off in the morning, do you:

**A** Help everyone else get ready: if they're on time, you're on time. ◯

**B** Get up, but attack anyone who dares look at you before you've showered? ⬡

**C** Run straight downstairs for breakfast! It's the most important meal of the day. ◯

**D** Urgh! The morning. You'll stay in bed! ◯

**E** You're already wide awake and ready for what the day has in store. ⬡

## 2 If you could have a superpower, what would it be?

**A** The ability to duplicate things. ◯

**B** Teleportation. ◯

**C** You can make all food – even vegetables – taste like chocolate. ◯

**D** You can make other people shapeshift. ◯

**E** Who needs a super power when you have good friends protecting you? ⬡

## 3 What is your ideal Sunday?

**A** Spending time with friends and family, helping them with whatever they need. ◯

**B** Going for a walk in the woods and generally avoiding people. ⬡

**C** Eating a Sunday roast. What else are Sundays for? ◯

**D** Sleeping in until sundown and then going out and making new friends. ◯

**E** Homework, of course. You won't succeed if you don't study. ◯

## 4. What is your favourite school subject?

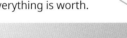

**A** PE – you love nothing more than running and fetching things. ⬡

**B** Physics – you love learning about space and how things move. ⬡

**C** Lunchtime – hey, it counts! No? Fine. Art – you love drawing apples. ⬡

**D** Drama – you love acting like someone else. ⬡

**E** Maths – you love crunching numbers and know what everything is worth. ⬡

## 5. How would your friends describe you?

**A** Helpful – always there when you need them. ⬡

**B** Friends? What friends? I don't need them. ⬡

**C** Funny – always cracking jokes at lunchtime. ⬡

**D** Loyal – once you've made a friend, they're your friend for life. ⬡

**E** Smart – always knows the right answer. ⬡

## MOSTLY A'S

### ALLAY

You love doing things for others and are always the most useful person in a room. You have a sunny personality and people love having you as a friend.

## MOSTLY B'S

### ENDERMAN

So you're a bit shy, and maybe even a little grouchy, but despite being a lone wolf, no one would dare pick a fight with you as they'd surely lose!

## MOSTLY C'S

### PIG

You are happiest when spending time with friends – around a dinner table, of course – and you love to share your passion for food with those around you.

## MOSTLY D'S

### ZOMBIE

You want everyone to be just like you – you're awesome, after all! You have a big group of friends who all like similar things and you love being part of a pack.

## MOSTLY E'S

### VILLAGER

You are a driven individual who loves a routine and is an active member of the community. You get on with everyone and know how to reach your goals.

# MARKETPLACE

DISCOVER
WITH NOOR

If you're looking to shake things up, then check out Minecraft Marketplace. You can embark on adventures with new maps and mini-games, mix up the look of your game with a texture pack, or maybe you just want an epic new style for your avatar. Here are some of our new favourites for you to try!

## TEXTURE PACKS Change the look of your game with a texture pack!

### LO-BIT 8-BIT
TETRASCAPE

How cute is this texture pack, which transforms your world into a pastel haven? It even comes with its own soundtrack, so you can get fully immersed. Definitely one to try!

### CUBED FRAMES TEXTURES
HEROPIXEL GAMES

If pastels aren't for you then what about the vibrant colours in this texture pack? With simple textures, this pack may trick you into thinking you're playing a different game entirely!

## MASH-UP PACKS Want a story and new textures to explore? Try a mash-up pack!

### VEHICLE MASHUP
ODYSSEY BUILDS

Who hasn't longed for a car to race across the Overworld in? In this mash-up, you have an entire city to explore to unlock loads of awesome vehicles to drive!

### UNICORN RANCH MASHUP
LIFEBOAT

This mash-up is truly magical! You get to craft your own baby unicorn and raise it. Once grown, you get to ride it around. And if that wasn't cool enough, they have magical powers!

# ADVENTURE MAPS

**Embark on a new adventure with these immersive maps!**

### DINOSAUR REBORN

KUBO STUDIOS

If you like dinosaurs, then you'll love this ROARsome new adventure! In this map, there are over 50 dinosaurs for you to breed, tame, fight, hatch and even ride.

### TOO MUCH HORROR!

CUBED CREATIONS

If horror is your cup of tea, then check out this adventure map, which is full of terrifying monsters and moments that will make you jump out of your skin. It's truly thrilling!

# MINI GAMES

**Looking for a fun new game to play within Minecraft? Try a mini game!**

### ONLY UP!

LIFEBOAT

If you're a cat person, then this mission may appeal to you: climb to the top of the obstacle course to save the cat at the summit. Told you! You'll be an expert at parkour by the top.

### NATURE SNAP

RAZZLEBERRIES

In this mini game, you get to explore the world, taking snaps of all the incredible wildlife, including lions, giraffes, elephants and many more animals. It's wild!

# SKINS

**Give your player characters a makeover with a new skin pack!**

### DUCKS SQUAD

VENIFT

You'll have a quacking time in these ducky skins! Who wouldn't want to look like an adorable yellow duckling in a fantastic outfit? Skin me up!

### CRIMSON TEENS

STREET STUDIOS

No one is more fashion-conscious than a teen. These super-cool teen outfits are all inspired by the cherry grove biome – arguably one of the most beautiful biomes in-game.

# WRITE YOUR OWN ADVENTURE

**WRITE**
WITH ARI

Put your creativity cap on and let's come up with an incredible adventure tale! Minecraft's full of story opportunities: you take part in a new adventure every time you play, after all!! Let's take some of those experiences and come up with an epic tale to share with your mates — or to play out the next time you load up the game!

## MAIN CHARACTER

First, you need to come up with your main character. This is who the story is going to be about. It could be you, or it could be someone entirely made-up – the choice is yours! Do they have a mob companion with them? It could be anything from a wolf to an allay.

**NAME** ................................................................

**WHAT DO THEY WANT?** ..................................................

................................................................

E.G. HERO OF THE VILLAGE, TO BE RICH WITH DIAMONDS, TOTEM OF UNDYING, TO BUILD A ZOO

**DRAW THEM HERE**

## ANTAGONIST

An antagonist is the enemy of your main character. They will usually mess up your main character's plans somehow or get in the way of them achieving their goals. They can be anything from a hostile mob to another player.

**NAME** ................................................................

**WHAT DO THEY WANT?** ..................................................

................................................................

**DRAW THEM HERE**

# BEGINNING

Every story has got to start somewhere! This is where you establish what your character wants, and begin their journey to get it.

......................................................................................................................................................
......................................................................................................................................................
......................................................................................................................................................
......................................................................................................................................................
......................................................................................................................................................
......................................................................................................................................................
......................................................................................................................................................

# MIDDLE

This is where things don't go to plan. Perhaps the antagonist has made an appearance and gets in the way of your character's goals. Before your character can get what they want, they must first deal with the issue. Does their companion help them or just make things worse?

......................................................................................................................................................
......................................................................................................................................................
......................................................................................................................................................
......................................................................................................................................................
......................................................................................................................................................
......................................................................................................................................................

# END

Your main character manages to defeat their foe and achieve the goal they set out to do.
Or not – it's your decision! Either way, all stories need a good ending!

......................................................................................................................................................
......................................................................................................................................................
......................................................................................................................................................
......................................................................................................................................................
......................................................................................................................................................
......................................................................................................................................................

The End!

# WOULD YOU RATHER ...

Put your decision skills to the test with these ridiculous Minecraft Would You Rathers! Sure, most of these wouldn't happen in the game, but wouldn't it be hilarious if they did? Which options will you choose? You could even ask your friends to see if they make the same decisions.

## YOU'VE MADE FRIENDS WITH A MOB, BUT IT ISN'T QUITE THE PET YOU'D IMAGINED.

Would you rather be followed around by a pig that eats all your crops every time you farm

OR

a goat that rams you off a cliff every time you try to take in a view?

## YOU'VE JUST DEFEATED A VILLAGE RAID AND START DREAMING ABOUT WHAT YOUR REWARD MIGHT BE.

Would you rather receive an inventory full of emeralds

OR

have a doting villager who bakes you cookies every day for the rest of your life?

## YOU'VE MANAGED TO INVENT A NEW POTION, BUT THE STATUS EFFECT ISN'T QUITE PERFECT.

Would you rather jump super far, but always crash your landing

### OR

become invisible on demand, but be stuck in armour that stays visible?

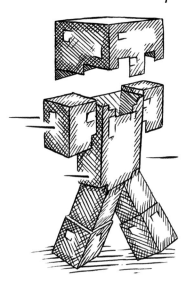

## YOU HAVE BIG PLANS FOR COLLECTING MOBS, BUT AREN'T SURE WHICH ONE TO GATHER.

Would you rather own an army of chickens that supply you with an endless supply of eggs (and the occasional chicken for dinner)

### OR

have an army of cats that keep creepers and phantoms at bay, as well as bringing you a bunch of occasionally nice gifts every morning?

## YOU'VE WOKEN UP TO FIND ONE OF YOUR NIGHTMARES HAS COME TO LIFE.

Would you rather Ender Dragons have broken through to the Overworld and are eating villagers for dinner

### OR

you're followed everywhere by a wandering tradesman who has started an acapella group with their llamas and never stops singing?

# BROWNIE BLOCKS

**BAKE**
WITH ARI

If you love chocolate brownies, you'll adore these blocky brownie bites! They're fudgy brownies with chocolate and coconut on top that will have friends and family – and maybe the odd hostile mob or two – flocking to your doors to have a bite. Roll up your sleeves and let's bake!

## INGREDIENTS

### BROWNIE
- 175 g unsalted butter
- 200 g dark chocolate
- 300 g caster sugar
- 150 g plain flour
- 3 eggs
- 100 g chocolate chips

### TOPPING
- 100 g milk chocolate
- 50 g desiccated coconut
- 1/2 tsp of green gel food colouring
- 1/2 tsp water

## TOOLS
- Plastic microwaveable bowl
- Large mixing bowl
- Wooden spoon
- Glass
- Rubber spatula
- Baking paper
- Baking tin – roughly 20 x 25 cm

**NEED GLUTEN FREE?**
Just switch out the plain flour for a gluten-free equivalent.

**NEED DAIRY FREE?**
Just make sure to use dairy-free butter, dark chocolate and chocolate chips.

## INSTRUCTIONS

### MIX

**STEP 1** Preheat your oven to 180°C / 160°C fan / gas mark 4.

**STEP 2** Pop your dark chocolate and butter into a microwaveable bowl. Ask an adult to help you microwave it in 30-second bursts, stirring between each one until the chocolate is fully melted.

**STEP 3** Put your melted chocolate into a mixing bowl and add the sugar. Stir together with a wooden spoon.

**STEP 4** Carefully measure your plain flour into your mixing bowl and mix it in.

**STEP 5** Grab a glass and crack your eggs into it, adding them to the mixture one at a time. Mix this up until it all combines to make a shiny, chocolatey batter.

**STEP 6** Now stir in your chocolate chips. If you don't have chocolate chips, you can add chocolate buttons or chop up a chocolate bar. Or leave them out!

**STEP 7** Line your tin with baking paper, making sure there's enough for the edges, too. Now pour your batter in and spread it out with your spoon or a spatula.

### BAKE

**STEP 8** Ask an adult to bake your brownies in the oven for 30–35 minutes. To know if your brownies are baked, insert a skewer or fork into the middle. If it comes out covered in uncooked batter, then it needs more time, but if it has some wet crumbs on it, then they're ready!

**STEP 9** Let your brownies rest in the tin until they are cool – this might take a while, so go ahead and read the rest of this annual while you wait.

**STEP 10** Once your brownies are cool, transfer them to a chopping board and ask an adult to cut them into small square pieces.

### DECORATE

**STEP 11** Now, if dirt blocks are what you're happy with, then you're done. But if you want to go one step further and make your brownies look like grass blocks, then read on. Melt your topping chocolate in your microwaveable bowl in 30-second bursts.

**STEP 12** Meanwhile, mix your water and gel food colouring together, then add to your coconut, stirring it and adding more colouring if needed until you get your desired green.

**STEP 13** Use a teaspoon to add a dollop of melted chocolate on top of each brownie bite.

**STEP 14** Now add a generous sprinkling of coconut on top.

**STEP 15** Admire for a second ... and then gobble them all up with your friends and family!

If you want to mix things up, why not change the colour of your coconut to purple and make mycelium blocks instead? Or you could leave the coconut white to look like a snow covered grass block!

# DELETED FEATURES

In the 15 years of Minecraft, we've seen countless new mobs, biomes and items added to the game. But if you've been a fan long enough, you may have spotted some things that were removed or discovered some mobs lurking in the code. How many of these have you seen?

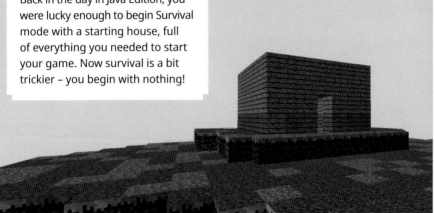

## STARTING HOUSE

Back in the day in Java Edition, you were lucky enough to begin Survival mode with a starting house, full of everything you needed to start your game. Now survival is a bit trickier – you begin with nothing!

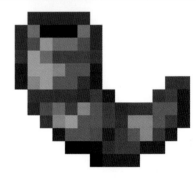

## COPPER HORN

This was essentially a funky-looking musical instrument that could play three sounds, depending on which direction you looked.

## NETHER REACTOR/ NETHER SPIRES

Once upon a time, you could build a Nether reactor. When activated, it would generate a huge Nether spire, full of items to collect.

## BUFFET

Two deleted world types are Caves and Floating Islands. In Caves, your entire Minecraft world was built within an enormous cave, while in Floating Islands, chunks of the Overworld were suspended in the air above you!

# UNUSED FEATURES

There are some unused mobs that never made it officially into the game, but still exist in the code. When you next play, why not try summoning them to see what happens?

## KILLER BUNNY
*Java only* Command: / summon rabbit ~ ~ ~ {RabbitType:99}
Cute rabbits not fun enough for you? Well, this one will certainly keep you on your toes – and maybe nibble on a few!

## ILLUSIONER
*Java only* Command: / summon illusioner
If pillagers, evokers and vindicators weren't challenging enough, you can summon the illusioner. This illager may look like it's about to crack out a crystal ball, but it has far more deadly weapons up its sleeves.

## GIANT ZOMBIE
*Java only* Command: / summon giant
You might want to think it through before summoning a giant zombie – for one, its name is no exaggeration, this mob really is massive!

## ZOMBIE HORSE
Command: /summon zombie_horse or use a spawn egg
Been dreaming of a green horse? I bet this isn't quite what you had in mind! You can either command or spawn this mob into being in Creative mode.

# SOMETHING SUS

Have suspicious sand and suspicious gravel slipped beneath your radar until now? Then where have you been hiding all this time? Grab a brush and let's get digging! Each suspicious block is like its own lucky dip — will there be something hiding within? Let's find out!

Warm Ocean

Cold Ocean

## WHERE DO I FIND THEM?

If you're in the desert, then keep an eye out for desert temples and wells. At the bottom of each, you'll find suspicious sand. You'll also find suspicious blocks in ocean ruins: sand if it's a warm ocean and gravel if it's cold. And lastly, you'll find suspicious gravel in trail ruins. These are structures built many moons ago, which have been buried underground over the years. They generate in some forested biomes, such as taiga, old growth and jungle biomes, and you'll only be able to see the tip above ground. So if you happen to stumble across some out-of-place blocks the next time you're ambling through the woods, you might find it rewarding to stop and dig down.

Desert Temple

Desert Well

Trail Ruins

## WHAT'S SUS ABOUT THEM?

These blocks aren't sus in a bad way, but they are hiding something. If you use a brush on a suspicious block, it will reveal an item within.

## BUT WHAT'S INSIDE?

All sorts! Commonly, you might find things including dyes, candles, seeds, coloured glass panes and hanging signs. But if you're really lucky, you'll find something rarer, such as a pottery sherd or a smithing template (see page 18).

## WHAT'S A POTTERY SHERD?

A pottery sherd by itself is fairly unremarkable, but craft four of them together and you'll have yourself a beautiful decorated pot. There are 20 different patterns to find across the Overworld, so what are you waiting for? Start searching!

# DECORATE A VILLAGE

Sure, villages come pre-decorated and you could just leave them well enough alone ... but where would be the fun in that?! Add your own creative flair and character to the villages in your Overworld with some of these exciting ideas. After all, why settle for what everyone else has?

**BUILDING**
WITH KAI

## BLACKSMITH

Want to upgrade your blacksmith from basic to epic? First, use a mixture of bricks and mud bricks to create an industrial-looking chimney, with a campfire surrounded by spruce trapdoors on top. You can elevate the style of the house by adding a new roof with stone bricks around the edges. Then add extra details such as barrels, chiselled stone bricks, stone buttons and a window ledge.

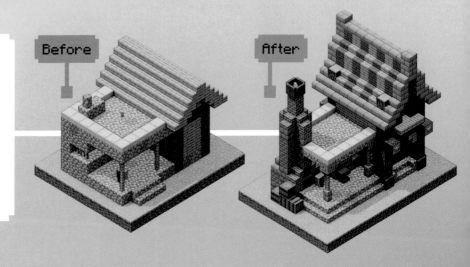

Before

After

Before

After

## WELL

Transform your standard village well into a wishing well! First, extend out your water area and surround it with a mixture of stone bricks, stone brick stairs and mossy stone brick stairs. Then add two pillars of oak logs, and build a pointed roof with oak stairs, stone brick stairs and stone bricks on top. Finish off with a stripped oak log on both sides and a stone button, and then you're ready to make a wish!

## FARM

Want to keep the pests out of your crops? Why not protect your farm creatively? Swap out the oak log sides for cobblestone stairs and mossy cobblestone stairs, then pop a composter on every corner. Next, add oak fences around the outside with little arches using oak slabs and oak fences above two oak fence gates. Finish off with a few lanterns perched on your fences. So cute!

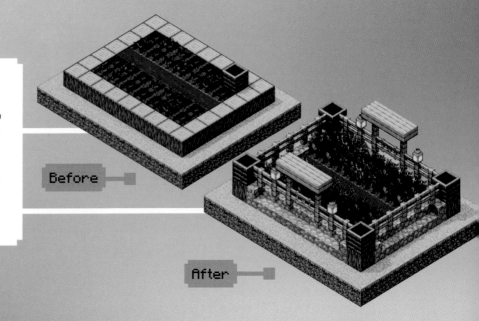

Before

After

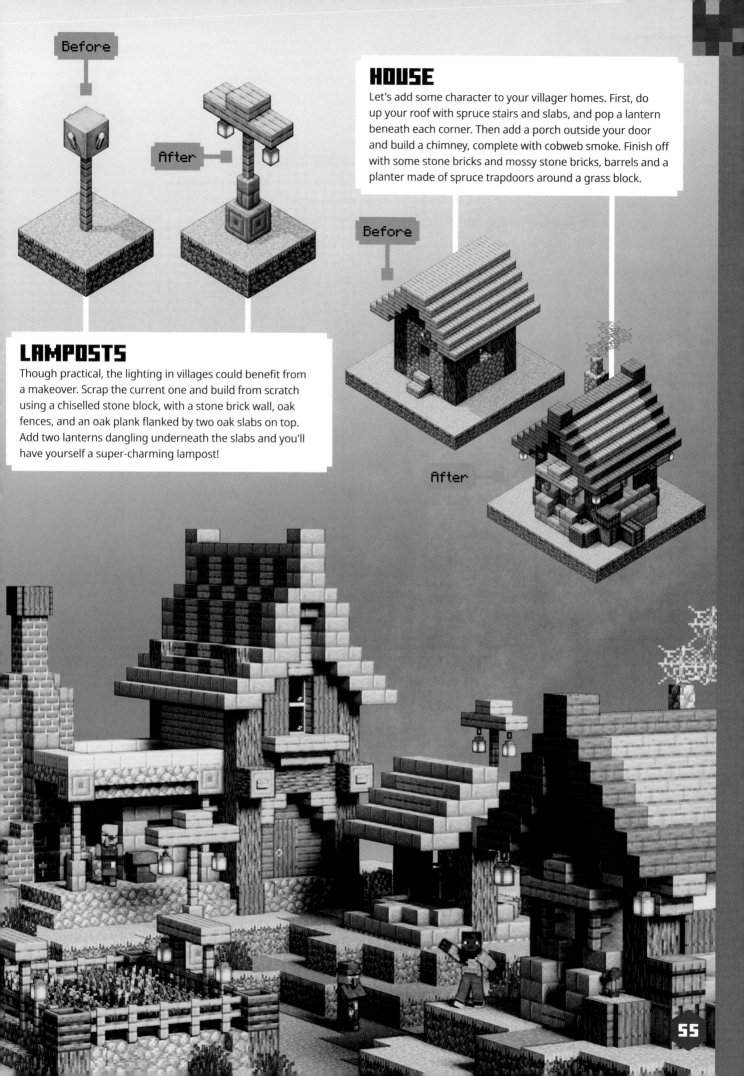

**Before**

**After**

## HOUSE

Let's add some character to your villager homes. First, do up your roof with spruce stairs and slabs, and pop a lantern beneath each corner. Then add a porch outside your door and build a chimney, complete with cobweb smoke. Finish off with some stone bricks and mossy stone bricks, barrels and a planter made of spruce trapdoors around a grass block.

**Before**

## LAMPOSTS

Though practical, the lighting in villages could benefit from a makeover. Scrap the current one and build from scratch using a chiselled stone block, with a stone brick wall, oak fences, and an oak plank flanked by two oak slabs on top. Add two lanterns dangling underneath the slabs and you'll have yourself a super-charming lampost!

**After**

# WORDSEARCH

Hold up a second, is that terracotta over there in the jungle? What's that doing there? And wait. There's more beneath! Keep on digging through this wordsearch and see what blocks you can find in the trail ruins beneath the surface, and fill them in below.

| A | M | S | C | X | D | I | R | T | X | S | G | K | C | P |
|---|---|---|---|---|---|---|---|---|---|---|---|---|---|---|
| E | B | U | H | O | N | P | E | Y | F | N | L | X | O | A |
| S | G | S | D | M | J | G | T | I | B | X | A | F | A | I |
| T | D | P | R | B | X | O | K | R | I | E | Z | J | R | X |
| O | K | I | F | G | R | A | V | E | L | O | E | G | S | C |
| N | L | C | S | G | S | I | R | X | L | B | D | M | E | H |
| E | C | I | L | N | A | X | C | B | Y | C | T | F | D | R |
| B | E | O | D | C | K | S | L | K | H | M | E | X | I | A |
| R | J | U | M | H | Z | T | I | A | S | D | R | D | R | L |
| I | B | S | T | O | N | E | G | D | T | A | R | H | T | Y |
| C | I | G | O | E | B | P | X | F | N | R | A | G | M | S |
| K | H | R | G | A | L | H | P | O | L | X | C | Y | N | F |
| S | P | A | C | O | B | B | L | E | S | T | O | N | E | O |
| F | C | V | J | T | E | R | R | A | C | O | T | T | A | J |
| K | M | E | I | D | X | E | A | J | X | G | T | C | Z | T |
| B | T | L | P | O | A | R | L | B | R | S | A | N | K | E |

## THINGS YOU'VE FOUND

- ☐ S_____ G_____
- ☐ T_____
- ☐ M__ B_____
- ☐ G_____
- ☐ G_____ T_____
- ☐ S____
- ☐ S____ B_____
- ☐ C_____
- ☐ D___
- ☐ C_____ D___

Check your answers on page 68

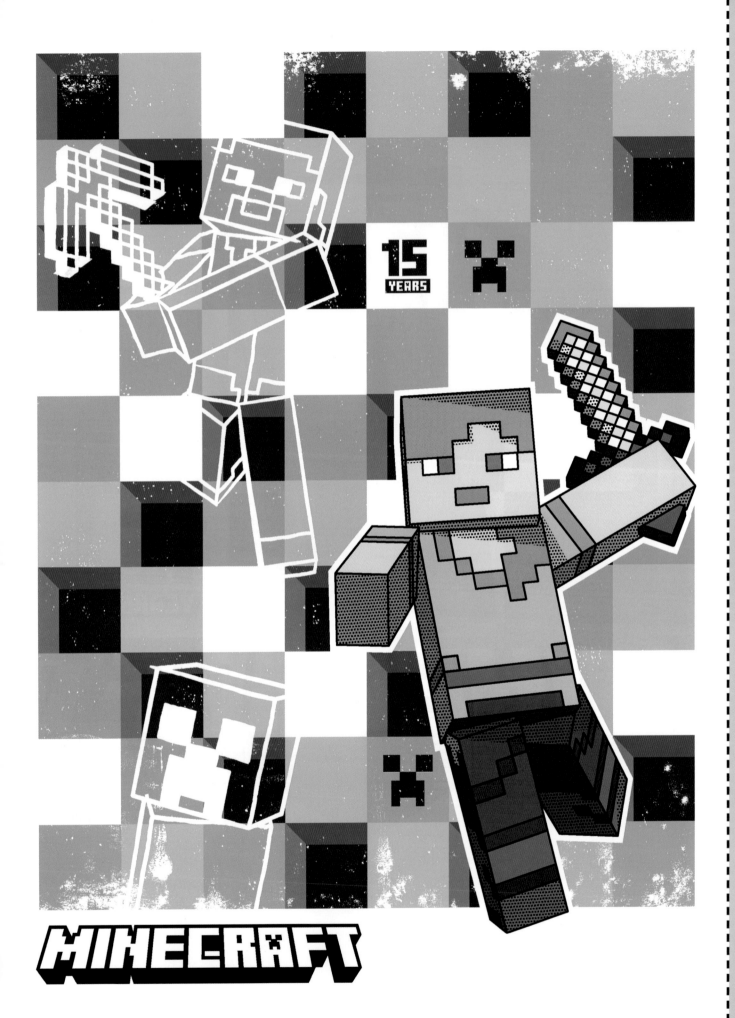

MINECRAFT

# ACTIVITY
# SUDOKU

Oh wow, there's suspicious gravel in these trail ruins! I wonder what we'll find if we use our brushes on them? Use your 'brush' to fill in this puzzle, making sure that each item appears only once in every box and line.

PUZZLES WITH STEVE

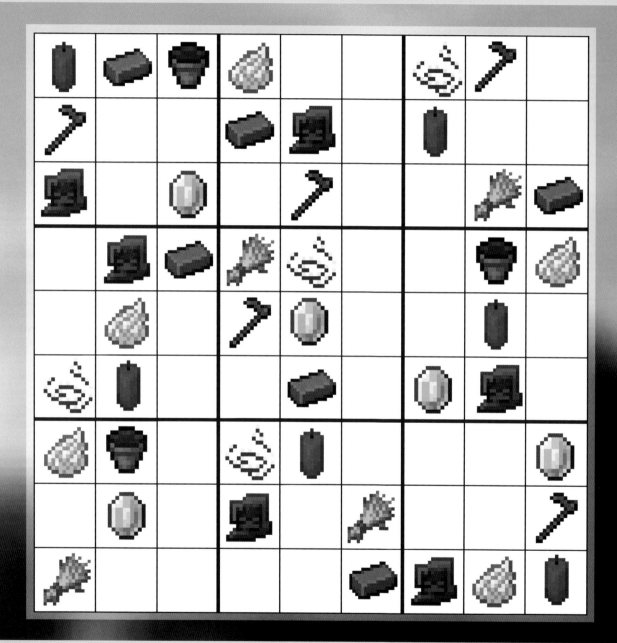

## KEY
If you don't want to draw the items, use the numbers in this key instead.

 1    2    3    4    5    6    7    8    9

Check your answers on page 68

# COMMUNITY CREATIONS

Minecraft has one of the biggest – and BEST – communities, with people from all over the world sharing their discoveries and creations. We are always endlessly inspired by your builds, and here are just some of the creations that caught our eye this year. What will you build next?

**DISCOVER**
WITH NOOR

## WHIMSICAL WINDMILL
### BY SPARKLEEGG

'Netherrack can be a fairly tricky block to build with, but I found that it looks great in addition to mangrove wood. Then just add some cherry wood, spruce wood and mud bricks, and you have yourself a really nice block palette.' How idyllic is this build?! We'd love to move in here. What blocks can you combine to create a similar look in your builds?

## ENCHANTMENT LIBRARY
### BY AUDIIBEE

'I wanted to create a simple and pretty way to make use of random caves. I used a lot of bookcases and lanterns to achieve the cosy look.' We love how imaginative this build is – who'd have thought a cave could be transformed into such a magical library? It makes you wonder what else caves could be used for!

## HISTORIC STREET

BY CLAIRE1593

'I used a variety of blocks based on how I wanted each building to look. I was inspired by the buildings in the city of Vienna, Austria.' It certainly transported us there! These buildings showcase the incredible detail you can add with the use of stairs, walls, slabs and fences. Where to build next?

## MUSHROOM MANOR

BY KATZIL

'I created this build to make my world a little more cottagecore. Using mushroom blocks for the roof, I added in spruce beams to complement this and with dark oak accents, it made the perfect block palette.' We love the warm colours of this build and all the cute details – how adorable are those hanging flower pots?! Why don't you try to incorporate mushroom blocks into your next build?

## SOUP HQ

BY BRINGMESOUP

'I wanted to build my future office building where me and my friends can create content together. So this build means a lot to me – one day you will see me here! This build also consists of many neutral colours and it took me about one hour to build.' Isn't it incredible that a build that first took form in Minecraft might one day be built in the real world? We love how modern and sleek this build is – so clever!

# HOW TO SURVIVE A VILLAGE RAID

EXPERT GUIDE
WITH EFE

Village raids sound like pure chaos, and they are! But whether you're looking for a challenge or you trigger one accidentally, knowing what to expect and how to conquer one is valuable knowledge indeed. Let's take a look!

## WHAT IS A VILLAGE RAID?

A village raid is an event triggered by the player, in which groups of illagers raid a village to defeat all the villagers – and you. If every villager is defeated, then the raid is over and you have lost.

## HOW ARE THEY TRIGGERED?

If you defeat a pillager captain, you will receive the Bad Omen status effect. Should you then enter a village with this, a raid will be triggered.

## WHAT HAPPENS?

As soon as you enter a village, a gang of angry pillagers will turn up to avenge their captain. A bar will appear at the top of your screen, which will indicate how many mobs you've got to defeat until that wave is over. There are multiple waves of village raids, getting progressively more difficult with mobs such as witches, evokers, vindicators and ravagers turning up for the party.

## HOW MANY WAVES WILL YOU HAVE TO SURVIVE?

The number of waves you need to battle depends on which difficulty mode you're on:

**PEACEFUL = 0     EASY = 3**
**NORMAL = 5     HARD = 7**

## CAN IT BE AVOIDED?

Actually, yes! If you've defeated a pillager captain and you don't want to trigger a raid, then all you have to do is drink some milk before entering a village.

## SO WHY WOULD YOU GO AHEAD WITH ONE?

The rewards, duh! If you survive a village raid, you'll be heavily rewarded by the villagers with the Hero of the Village status effect, which will see discounts applied to all of your villager trades. I hope you stocked up on emeralds! Not only that, they'll put on a celebratory firework display in your honour and shower you with gifts to show their appreciation. Lucky for you, they clearly haven't figured out that you started the raid in the first place. Shh, we won't tell them if you don't!

## AND THE BEST BIT?

Every time you defeat an evoker during the raid, they'll drop a totem of undying. This crafty item will allow you to cheat death if you have it to hand!

## HOW CAN YOU PREPARE YOURSELF?

To truly ace this battle, fill your inventory with as many things on this list as you can:

- STRONG ARMOUR, INCLUDING A SHIELD, PLUS SPARES
- SPARE BLOCKS
- BOWS AND PLENTY OF ARROWS
- A STRONG SWORD - OR TWO
- A BED
- BOATS
- IRON INGOTS
- IRON BLOCKS
- PUMPKINS
- FIREWORK LAUNCHER
- FOOD - YOU WON'T HAVE MUCH TIME TO EAT, SO PACK FOODS WITH HIGH NUTRITION VALUES, SUCH AS COOKED PORKCHOPS OR GOLDEN CARROTS
- POTIONS OF REGENERATION
- PLENTY OF EMERALDS FOR AFTERWARDS

# SURVIVING A VILLAGE RAID

## SO, HOW DO YOU BOSS THIS FIGHT?

Protect your villagers. Get them to head indoors by ringing a bell, then use whatever blocks are in your inventory to block up their doors and keep them inside. This will keep them safe from the raiding mobs.

## BUILD AN ARMY

Use iron blocks and pumpkins to create as many iron golems as you can. These will help you defend the village.

## USE AN EXPLOSIVE WEAPON

If you want to hit multiple mobs at the same time, a firework launcher might be the best answer! Just make sure you're not too close, so you don't get caught in the fire.

## HEAL YOUR IRON GOLEMS

If you notice your iron golems start to crack, just use iron ingots on them to restore them back to full health.

## TRAP VINDICATORS IN BOATS

Got a vindicator running at you? Chuck a boat in front of them and they'll get trapped in there, where they won't be able to hit you and you can defeat them with no fear.

**REMEMBER TO SLEEP**
A village raid isn't over quickly – there's a good chance that night will fall during it. If you don't want to be fighting illagers AND all the other hostile mobs of the night, you best find yourself a safe spot far enough away from hostile mobs to sleep the night away. At the very least, you'll want to set your respawn point in the village, so you don't wind up somewhere super far away if you're defeated.

**JUMP INTO THE FRAY**
Get out your sword or axe and run headfirst into battle ... if you're brave enough. If you act fast enough, you should be able to get your hits in before pillagers have had time to draw back their crossbows.

# MOB QUIZ

So you think you're an expert in mobs? Sure, you may be able to tell a zombie from a drowned and a stray from a skeleton, but do you know what each mob drops? Let's put your knowledge to the test! Pair each mob with what they have a chance of dropping below.

GHAST

BLAZE

**A** SEA GRASS

**B** POPPIES

**C** GLASS BOTTLE

**D** TRIDENT

DROWNED

WITHER SKELETON

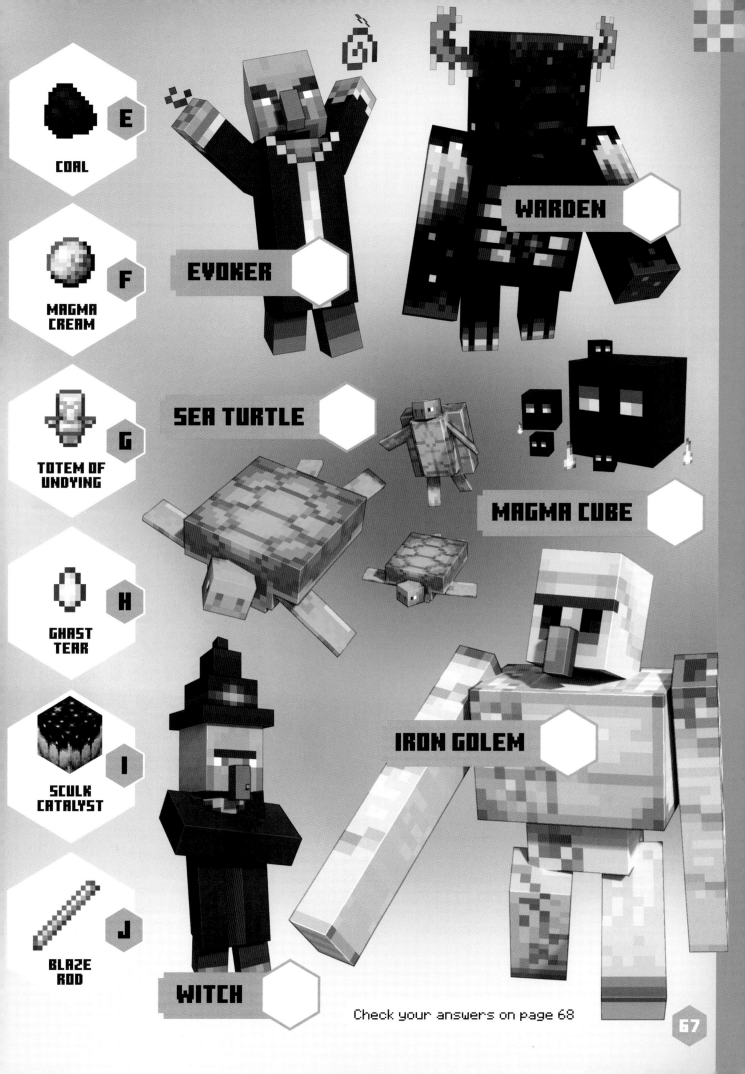

COAL **E**

MAGMA CREAM **F**

TOTEM OF UNDYING **G**

GHAST TEAR **H**

SCULK CATALYST **I**

BLAZE ROD **J**

EVOKER

WARDEN

SEA TURTLE

MAGMA CUBE

IRON GOLEM

WITCH

Check your answers on page 68

# ANSWERS

## 16-17

## 24-25

## 56

| A | M | S | C | X | D | I | R | T | X | S | G | K | C | F |
|---|---|---|---|---|---|---|---|---|---|---|---|---|---|---|
| E | B | U | H | O | N | P | E | Y | F | N | L | X | O | A |
| S | G | S | D | M | J | G | T | I | B | X | A | F | A | I |
| T | D | P | A | B | X | O | K | R | I | E | Z | J | R | X |
| O | K | I | F | G | R | A | V | E | L | O | E | G | S | C |
| N | L | C | S | G | S | I | R | X | L | B | D | M | E | H |
| E | C | I | L | N | A | X | C | B | Y | C | T | F | D | R |
| B | E | O | D | C | K | S | E | K | H | M | E | X | I | A |
| R | J | U | M | H | Z | T | I | A | S | D | R | D | R | L |
| I | B | S | T | O | N | E | G | D | T | A | R | H | T | Y |
| C | I | G | O | E | B | P | X | F | N | R | A | G | M | S |
| K | H | R | G | A | L | H | P | O | L | X | C | Y | N | P |
| S | P | A | C | O | B | B | L | E | S | T | O | N | E | O |
| F | C | V | J | T | E | R | R | A | C | O | T | T | A | J |
| K | M | E | I | D | X | E | A | J | X | G | T | C | Z | T |
| B | T | L | P | O | A | R | L | B | R | S | A | N | K | E |

SUSPICIOUS GRAVEL
TERRACOTTA
MUD BRICKS
GRAVEL
GLAZED
TERRACOTTA

STONE
STONE BRICKS
COBBLESTONE
DIRT
COARSE DIRT

## 59

(image grid of item icons)

## 66-67

1. GHAST - **GHAST TEAR**
2. BLAZE - **BLAZE ROD**
3. DROWNED - **TRIDENT**
4. WITHER SKELETON - **COAL**
5. EVOKER - **TOTEM OF UNDYING**
6. WARDEN - **SCULK CATALYST**
7. SEA TURTLE - **SEA GRASS**
8. MAGMA CUBE - **MAGMA CREAM**
9. WITCH - **GLASS BOTTLE**
10. IRON GOLEM - **POPPIES**

# GOODBYE

Wow, what a fantastic year it's been –
I can't wait for the next one! We'll see you
again soon to share all the exciting things
we're currently working on. Thanks so
much for playing!

Jay Castello
Mojang Studios

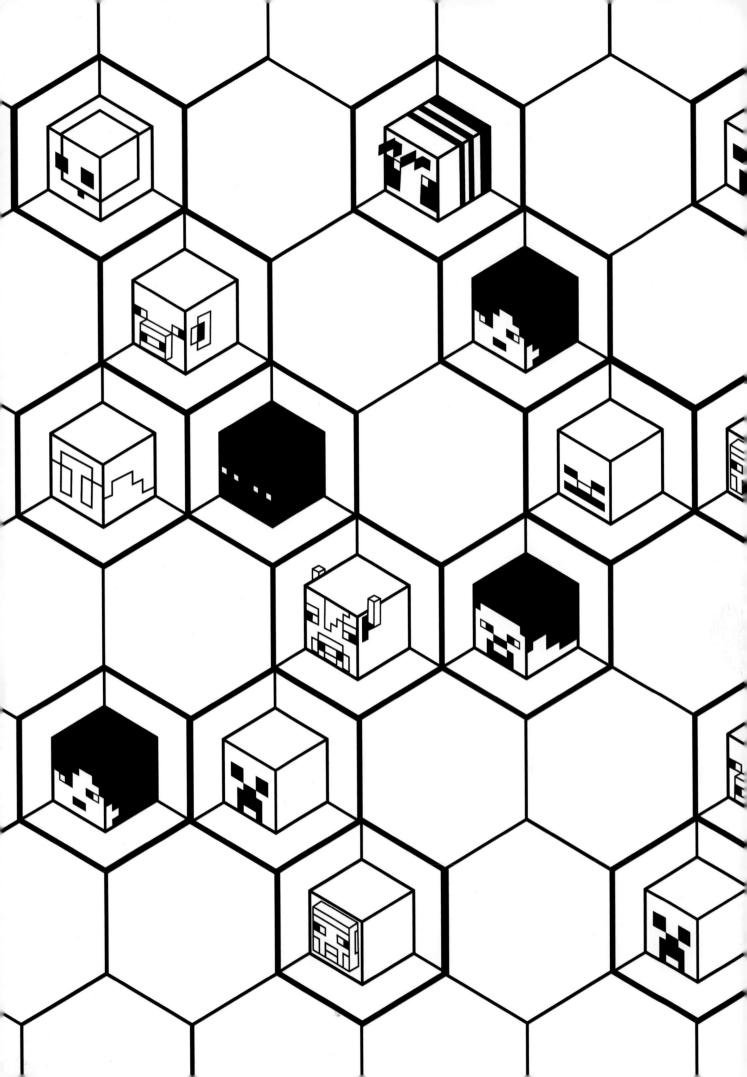